COURAGE
MY LOVE

Books by Merle Shain

COURAGE MY LOVE

SOME MEN ARE MORE PERFECT THAN OTHERS

WHEN LOVERS ARE FRIENDS

HEARTS THAT WE BROKE LONG AGO

COURAGE MY LOVE

A book to light an honest path

Merle Shain

BANTAM BOOKS
TORONTO • NEW YORK • LONDON • SYDNEY • AUCKLAND

COURAGE MY LOVE

A Bantam Book / February 1989

Grateful acknowledgement is made for permission to reprint lyrics from:
"You Can Call Me Al" by Paul Simon, copyright © 1986 Paul Simon. Used
by permission. "Me And Bobby McGee" by Kris Kristofferson and Fred
Foster, copyright © 1969 COMBINE MUSIC CORPORATION. All rights
controlled and administered by SBK BLACKWOOD MUSIC INC. All rights
reserved. International copyright secured. Used by permission.
Cover: Wallpaper design by William Morris.
Courtesy of Clarkson N. Potter, Inc.

Book design by M 'N O Production Services, Inc.

Library of Congress Cataloging-in-Publication Data

Shain, Merle.
  Courage my love.

  1. Love. I. Title.
BF575.L8S516   1989   152.4   88-47835
ISBN 0-553-05334-5 (pbk.)

PRINTED IN THE UNITED STATES OF AMERICA

DH   0 9 8 7 6 5 4 3 2 1

For my mother

Ah Love! could thou and I with Fate conspire
To grasp this sorry Scheme of things entire.
 Would not we shatter it to bits—and then
Re-mould it nearer to the Heart's Desire!

From the *Rubáiyát* of Omar Khayyám

Contents

Part One
LONGING

Roaming with a hungry heart

A man told me once of leaving his wife for a woman from Bloomington, Indiana. His wife was pregnant and near the end of term, and the woman from Bloomington, Indiana, was somebody else's wife and some other small person's mother. What's more he did not know her, but he saw her standing out on a dock at twilight and he said, "There is the one!"

How did he know? you ask. How did he know that a woman whose silhouette he could barely make out in the dusk was worth his putting his family at risk and his life into chaos? He didn't of course, but those were questions he never asked. So strong was the pull, so great his need, it was as if he was sucked into the eye of the storm against his will, and he was powerless to do anything about it.

The fantasy is to the fulfillment what the mirage is to the oasis, but when the need is great all other destinations are cancelled and it's every man for himself. Even now when I tell you not to trust in this I can feel your resistance through the page. Just as I feel mine.

Who among us has not been blindsided by self-delusion, tempted by deprivation, and like the man in the story, found himself crawling on his belly in the desert toward a figment of his imagination that isn't even there?

Who has not confused the present for the past, the daylight for the dream, their loneliness for their salvation, an ordinary person for a king or queen? Who has not searched for the human being who should have been there but did not come? Certainly not I.

It will be a hard sell if you try to separate love from illusion, to put emotional incontinence in rubber pants, I tell myself. Who do you expect to buy a book that tells people why they should give up a drug they've always been told is good for them? When what they really want to read is one that tells them where to get more of it, and how to keep the cost from going up?

You want to tackle our whole "love will save you" mythology, to call the romantic love tradition a deep and dirty lie? You think you can stem the seepage, keep your readers from pissing themselves away on dreams?

You and who else? I ask myself.

Well, me with a little help from them, comes the answer. But it will take quite a bit of help from them.

Some say the longing we feel is for the symbiosis we once had with our mothers in the womb, and our inordinate need to bond our sense of being incomplete on our own, akin to phantom pains in a missing limb.

It's not surprising, when you think of it, that we would incline yearningly to our prenatal life with its room service and temperature controls, considering that first off in the real world we have to face our dependence on the frustrating and inconsistent breast. Which is why psychoanalysts believe that if a baby has a good relationship with the breast he grows up to feel gratitude and learns to love. But if the breast eludes him as often as it gives him succor and relief, he feels anger and fear and learns envy and guilt and hate.

The mother, after all, is the baby's first love object, and nursing is his first affair, so if he ends up having to beg for what he needs, he learns more than just not to love, he learns to fear needing love, and to resent anyone who has that power over him. And when you consider how dependent a baby is on his mother and that her love is for him a matter of life or death, this isn't an overreaction. It seems under the circumstances really quite slight.

In any case, when you fear needing love, but need it just the same, it gives you, when you get it, not only pleasure but also pain. And if you also resent the person who is holding you in their embrace and consider it a grasp, you aren't likely to stay long or give much back.

Perhaps that explains why we have a bulimic society gorging and purging itself on relationships while everyone walks around undernourished, looking for someone else.

There is a Wintu tale from California about a Coyote and a Toad. Coyote had Toad for a wife. He beat her so regularly that she had warts on her back. So at night Coyote would creep away looking for new girls.

One evening he heard of a dance a long way off. Under the pretext of hunting, Coyote went and danced, and saw a girl all painted up. This excited him. He sang a song asking her to be his partner. They danced together, and made love behind the bushes.

In the morning Coyote woke and saw that the girl was Toad. He felt miserably tricked: Coyote beat Toad so much that her wrists went limp.

"I am a lover and have not found my thing to love," said Sherwood Anderson and the man who left his wife for the woman from Bloomington. "I drank at every vine/The last was like the first/I came upon no wine/So wonderful as thirst" was how Edna St. Vincent Millay put it.

It is out of that inaccessible tower of the past that longing leers and beckons and why we blame the failure of love rather than ourselves. It is why we search in vain and come to think that love is pain. And why broken hearts are one of the few growth industries in these depressed times.

Which is to say yearning is a deficiency condition, on the order of pellagra or beriberi, caused as they are by not having consumed enough of what one needs, in this case, love. And the resulting fracture in the personality can be reversed, or it can be allowed to worsen, and the choice is yours. Emotional hemophiliac, lone ranger, don juan, healed and happy? Which will you choose to be? Will you choose yearning which is hunger or love which is food?

A reporter once told me of asking an artist, whose painting showed a man with a lantern knocking on a door that had no doorknob, why he hadn't finished the painting, and the artist had replied, "That is the door to the human heart. A door handle would be useless. The human heart can be opened only from the inside."

2

When love throws a light on you

I met a man once who had just separated from his wife and talked endlessly about how upsetting life with her had been. "We could never discuss anything without her flying off the handle," he confided. "She even hit me when she lost her temper, and recently the police picked me up when the neighbors reported they saw us fighting in the car. That's when I knew it was time to throw in the towel." He looked tired when he told me this, and terribly sad. And I felt sorry for him, even wondered how such a lovely man could have had such a person for his mate. And then one evening when I'd only known him a month or two he took a swing in my direction, screaming as he raised his arm, "Why is it that all the angry women find their way to me?"

It's always easier to see another's behavior and judge it than to ask if some of it might be caused by us. Always easier to think we married the wrong person instead of wondering if we might be the wrong person ourself.

I often think we get so mad at the person we tried to love and who tried to love us because the failure of those attempts reminds us of our having fumbled before. We've been waiting for that healing love so long and now this person here has teased us into remembering our neediness and then blown it and we're madder than hell. In any case, they get charged with the national debt even if we just met them last week.

Love is supposed to make us feel whole and happy, rich and beautiful and even thin, and if it doesn't we think we married the frog instead of the prince and take steps to trade him in. When someone really loves you, you are supposed to feel like the fairest one in the land, and if you don't, you think it is their fault, because your beauty is in their eye.

"Nobody ever loved anybody like everybody wants to be loved," Mignon McLaughlin once wrote, and she was surely right. We expect a lot from love—often a lot more than we expect from ourselves.

Saul Bellow's character Henderson the Rain King, although rich and married for the second time, keeps hearing a voice deep inside himself saying, "I want, I want, I want." He is disgusted with himself. Even when he is playing checkers with his children and he wants to let them win, he jumps all over the board yelling, "King me, King me," and he can't stop himself. Some people, he muses, seem to find satisfaction in being. Others are taken up with becoming. "Becoming" people are very unlucky, always in a tizzy. He was, he knew, unfortunately a becoming person. "Becoming," he concludes, was beginning to come out of his ears.

Finally he goes off to Africa, a country he hopes will help him to find out what it is he wants so badly. On his arrival in Africa standing alone by a thatched hut he says to no one in particular, "Lily, my after-all dear wife, wanted us to end each other's solitude. Now she was no longer alone, but I still was, and how did that figure?"

At some level we sense it is a personal matter, this business of becoming, but still we hold love responsible. We want more love and admiration, more intimacy and ecstasy, more power and more glory, more sex and more amusement. And don't forget more room to maneuver and more support.

Even when we could give love a hand, we don't.

It's love we expect to give us a hand, so we sit there and wait for it, or call it bad names and cry. And like dogs, we hunt in dreams.

A friend of mine, who is a crisis worker in a school system, a job which means that if a student is about to stab the principal she's the one who jumps between them, and also the single parent of two sons, was shopping with me in a farmer's market one Saturday morning when a sleeping baby went by carried aloft on his father's warm chest. "Get out of there this minute," she hissed at the baby, "and let me get in!" Then we both broke up, till we broke down.

It would be nice, God knows, to be the apple of someone's eye. To have your needs respected and thought valid, your person treasured and admired, even maybe your body lusted for and desired. To be number one, the favored child.

Psychoanalysts feel that needing someone to adore you twenty-four hours a day is arrested development left over from not getting the adoration from your mother you had a right to when you were young. And all those people we call narcissists are those children who seek admiration to counter their inner feelings of emptiness but have not anything of their own to give.

"The real beloved is the empty self," Kierkegaard said, and of course he was right. Because when the self is empty there is no surplus love to give, so seeking love is all such an empty self is capable of, and the only interest it has.

"It may be called the Master Passion, the hunger for self-approval," Mark Twain wrote, understanding so well that all life's a search for our own admiration and other people can only help out till the right thing comes along.

Sometimes it is said that love doesn't last, and anyone expecting to find happiness should expect the trouble they get. And sometimes it is said that everyone has a bag packed for the big one should it happen along. But I know I have heard more exit lines in my short life than I am able to quote, and they all add up to the same thing. "I am not happy, so the problem must be you." Which is, when you think of it, kind of a bum rap to lay on love.

My son once came home from nursery school and said, "Mrs. Darling put her hand on Ethan's head, but she didn't put her hand on mine." And I replied, probably stirring the soup or otherwise only half concentrating, "Maybe Ethan needs reassurance." "What's 'ssurance?" he asked. "Well you know, maybe Ethan didn't feel good about himself so he needed a little extra love." "Will you tell Mrs. Darling I don't feel good about myself," he responded without a moment's thought.

We are all the same, whether we are five or forty-five. We just learn to hide it a little better. This "becoming" business is tough work. For some, it takes a lifetime. But it is your own love you are looking for, not anybody else's. Of that I am perfectly certain.

You might find a Mrs. Darling to make you feel good about yourself or you could adore someone whom others admire, thinking by association to look good yourself. And you can look the country over, searching for someone who sees the person you want to believe you are, but in the end, if you don't give yourself approval they won't be able to do anything much for you, no matter how much they try.

So many people use other people to court themselves and then, when it ends, speak of all they did for love. And the women's magazines tell them how, selling control in every issue on how to get and keep a man, while a genre of self-help literature grows up around us, to speak to those suffering from thin love in the way we once suffered from thin blood.

But people are not poultices that one can put upon one's wounds, and love has nothing to do with using others as positive reflectors so you can think well of yourself. Or of trying desperately to make another do what best suits your needs, as if somehow their life was yours as well, and no one but you had needs. And as for selling yourself, well, you may have a short-term yield but you'll show no long-term profits because narcissism, which masquerades as love, and self-love too, is still anxiety, not love, whatever you want to call it.

And as long as we think we have to have somebody to adore us to be somebody, we are stuck in a holding pattern, whining and waiting, impotent and injured, blaming those who have failed us, not knowing we are complicitous in keeping ourselves from becoming the persons we are meant to be.

And as long as we think we need love to make us something more than we are alone, and when it doesn't, it isn't love, the one who doesn't love is ourself. With friends like us who needs enemies? Or one might say, with enemies like us what hope is there for love?

A lot of people try to bludgeon love and admiration from another in order to give it to themselves, passing off P.R. for empathy, promissory notes for capital investments, doubts for deeds, but in the end it is easier if you give direct because until you do, nobody much is fooled. And certainly not yourself.

There isn't a perfect person somewhere, only a more perfect person we might become, and there isn't a paradise someone can lead us to unless it's the world we make for ourselves when we stop expecting it to be delivered by someone else.

You can think you must look still for the perfect one, or that the best one got away, or that love is a fraud and a failure and that you want it not, or that everything went wrong because your mother didn't love you, but the one you wait for is yourself. "The world was always yours," Archibald MacLeish wrote. "You would not take it. Reach out your hand to yourself and it is yours."

3

Behold the dreamer cometh

I knew a couple once, I say once, because as a couple they no longer exist, who were young and in love and planning their lives. Then one day she found a letter he had written to a woman in California saying he would meet her two weeks hence, by which time he would have left his wife.

The wife packed her bag and left him a note, saying simply that she was going to a friend's, because she didn't want him to watch her falling apart. When he called, begging her to stay, she said, "I can't give you what you want. You want to be in love all the time. It's not possible to have romance every day in a longstanding relationship. I can give you contentment and loyalty and enough security so you can grow. But I can't give you excitement, I can't promise to admire you each and every day. And while we would have, I hope, little renaissances along the way, there would not be that beating heart excitement which you seem to crave."

"Please don't leave me," he said, after a while. "If you go I will be truly lost. I realize now that you are the light I steer my boat by and the logbook in which I chart its course." She came back and stayed with him, till he left her for a dancer, but by then it wasn't just her, it was them.

"I need a photo opportunity. I want a shot at redemption," go the words of the Paul Simon song, and we sing along with him, just so many tourists here, as our relationships expire like parking meters and we let ourselves out the side door of our lives to go searching for the promised land.

It's hard to understand why it is that when we have roots we want wings and when we have wings we seek roots, or why it is so difficult to have both at the same time. I just know that the people making the change to get one when they have the other rarely realize how important the one they are giving up will be until they've lost it. But by then, it is too late.

It's odd that the highly perishable commodity, passionate love, with its limited shelf life, is thought a suitable foundation on which to hang the whole exhaustive structure of family and property and tradition but we rarely question it, although we often pay the price for not having done so.

Romantic love has its origins in courtly love and courtly love in religion, which is why we consider romantic love a higher calling to be answered regardless of other commitments and people who may be hurt. And why so many of us go through life longing for an experience that will give our life meaning and wholeness, and look for what we seek in love where once we sought for it in God.

Some say the ecstasy we find in the loved one is divine love and that the search for the perfect lover is just the search for our own soul. That when we fall in love, we project onto the other all our longing, all our loneliness, the sum total of our unconscious life, and that the other that we fall in love with is just the part of ourselves they enabled us to reach. Which is, I guess, why we call the loved one our soul mate and why Narcissus looked into the pool and fell in love with the image of himself. Why many prefer to love a phantom or someone they can't really have, rather than wake up in the morning beside a real body in the bed, and why, when life gets in the way of fantasy, we so often wander away.

There is a difference between a body mate and a soul mate and about that we should not be confused. The first is another person and the second an extension of ourselves. So while a love affair may start with romantic love, romance can never survive real life because it is a search for sacred love and sacred love is not of this world. And while we often try to find it by using the body as a conduit to the soul, and sometimes we find it for a short while, romantic love only thrives on longing and not getting what you need. Because it is yourself you are searching for through an elusive other and it is not possible to long for someone who is there.

And of course, there is something about everyday life with its everyday cares that changes a projection into a relation and the lover into a mate, and the soul mate becomes the body mate and love more human than divine. And then sometimes our soul search migrates into space and attaches itself to another and we follow it like a butterfly forgetting everything else.

It's always a puzzlement when someone leaves another to those who watch from the outside. How can we know when the shoe pinches who do not wear it? Who are we to judge another's stumblings who falter along ourselves? But sometimes when you watch a couple where someone leaves one person for another you know who is left and who is chosen has nothing to do with either one, only that the person who did the leaving is trying to stay faithful to their picture of themselves, and has forced themselves across the border to a place they have never been. And when we speak of those who go the course and those who want it all, we are not speaking of this person because there is no language that can be applied to them. And all that can be said of them is that in a kinder world a longing so great would have a valid claim.

I knew such a person who left a wife he adored, and a child he rejoiced in, for someone he'd just met. And those who knew them said they couldn't believe it because he'd always been so attentive, and was their idea of the perfect spouse. He was from an illustrious family, one of several children of a noble scion, and while his heritage lay about his shoulders like a mantle he tossed his head and appeared to take it lightly, preferring to make his own way and to set his own tests. He wanted to be a composer, and worked at it every day, his wife, who worked in the recording industry, giving him her support. And then one day he told her he wanted to do his share. "It's time to start a family," he said, "time for me to take a job."

He left them a year or so after that. The woman he chose was a star in his new field. And I know the cheap seats would say he traded up, replacing one woman for another the way men sometimes leave a pretty woman for an accomplished one and take bows for having grown.

But it seems to me that if he is to stand accused

of not loving it wasn't the women he didn't love so much as that he didn't love himself, although in the end that usually amounts to the same thing. Perhaps the message of his childhood was that he was not important in himself but only through those he was connected to, I cannot say for sure. I only know for him it was always important to be on a winning team. And that he loved the first wife when she made it possible for him to believe in himself as a musician, but needed something more when that dream deserted him. And even now as his second wife believes herself his heart's desire she is just supporting cast.

Because all that attentiveness to his family that people admire so much, and all those hymns to marriage that he so often sings, are only the evocations of a penitent hoping the gods will protect him from the night.

I know this story embodies some difficult truths, and there are those who will say I am too easy on him, and those who will say I am too hard, but what I am trying to say is simply this—this is romantic love for what it is, an infirm thing made of equal parts of hope and fraud. Call it an opiate, a petition, a malady, it is not anything of love.

Some people spend their life looking for their soul in other faces, not knowing that what they search for is themselves, or sensing that they are using love to link them to the great divine, as if it were a rocket ship not a roller coaster that climbs to adoration and sinks to disillusion and then scales the heights again.

Romantic love has highs and lows and lots of rare emotions and dangerous sensations but it bores easily and has no friendship in it, and often when it's over, it is as if a tornado passed. It's a very expensive form of recreation, a theater play with daydreams, a frolic of your own in which you are the main event, and on the whole, if I had to choose between being a body mate or a soul mate, I'd choose to be a body mate because there will be plenty of time to be soul mates in the next world and body mates are here and now.

Human love is based in every day, not fantasies or illusions. It acknowledges the other person as a separate person and even loves them for their imperfections, for their vulnerabilities and their incompleteness, and allows them to change and to grow. It seeks to honor, not to use, to empower, not to overpower, and when it fails, it just gets cranky, it does not blow a fuse.

There is an old Armenian fable William Saroyan adapted that goes like this. "A man had a cello with one string over which he drew the bow for hours at a time, holding his finger in one place. His wife endured this noise for seven months, waiting patiently for the man to either die of boredom or destroy the instrument. In as much as neither of these desirable things happened, however, one night she said, in a very quiet voice too, you may be sure, 'I have observed that when others play that magnificent instrument there are four strings over which to draw the bow, and the players move their fingers about continuously.' The man stopped playing for a moment, looked at his wife wisely, shook his head, and said, 'You are a woman. Your hair is long, your understanding short. Of course the others move their fingers about constantly. They are looking for the place. I've found it.'"

We, too, think we've found it. But the "it" we think we've found could use a reassessment. Romantic love doesn't make it as a search for love or a search for God. And as a search for self it does not do that either, half so well as we could do it for ourselves. When we project ourself onto another and fall in love with them, we haven't got us and we haven't got them, but when we repatriate ourself and offer a total self to another there is more of us to go around and a whole lot more of love.

The time has come to winnow out the desires that don't count from the ones that really matter. And to recognize that the hemlock in the nectar of narcissism is that we spend our lives alone. We have a common interest as human beings to come to the aid of human love because a world built on chimeras is not a world we can trust. And in that world we all seek, that world of gifts given and gifts received, that world where there is goodness of fit, where there is always someone to catch our fall, the name of trust goes hand in hand with love.

Part Two

THE OTHER

4

What is this thing called love?

For most people there seem to be three stages to love. The first stage is that Some Enchanted Evening kind of thing that everybody hankers for, when someone seems to loom out of the crowd as the only one that matters. This is the love of storybooks and songs, the bell-ringing, heart-in-the-mouth kind of love that people always long for, and like to believe is made in heaven. A choice guided by the gods and handed over to us fully formed.

The terrible truth is that such a choice is more often influenced by our subconscious, and the person we seek out, often a rerun of an earlier movie, generally a parent we hungered for as a child. And we come to that love dowered with the hopes and fears and needs of the past, none of which has anything to do with this person we have just met and hardly know, this Fig Newton of our imagination, this waltz around the room with our own ego, this human being who deserves better.

And like the riddle Lincoln was fond of asking—"If you call a tail a leg, how many legs has a dog? Five? No, calling a tail a leg doesn't make it a leg"—calling something love does not make it love.

Which brings me to the second stage of love, often short and not so sweet, when we find out they have clay feet. And worse they spot ours and point them out, putting an abrupt end to our fantasy life about ourselves. This is the stage when many people bail out, crying, "Saved by the bell!" and "Wasn't that a close call!" and "What did I see in him?"

But if you hang around long enough, you might just fall in love, and if you are very lucky, they might too. And both of you might look the other in the eye and say, as if seeing each other for the first time, "So it's you." Which is the third stage of love. Or you might say, the first stage, because the other two don't count for much, at least not with me.

The first stage lasts six weeks, "eight in spring," one wag said. The second can be as short as a phone call or as long as eternity depending on how neurotic you are, but the third is what you are waiting for, the real gift, not from the gods, but from yourself.

How do I get from here to there, I hear you say, and I must answer. I am not sure I know. Just that there are many turns upon the road and none of them are marked. And they all take that peculiar kind of fear people call courage and a little bit of luck, if you are to stumble into grace and find the miracle of your altered heart.

But this I can tell you and I know that it is true. There can't be a we until there is an I to keep company with the thou, as Martin Buber explained so well, and if the thou is only someone chosen to service your discontent, or is simply an extension of yourself, there can never be a we and you are alone. Because the love to which Buber was pointing with a finger grows when you give of yourself to another and when you give from this good place, you find you love yourself as well. And while it's often easier to flesh someone out with your own creativity and fall in love with what you've made, the real joy is in understanding and accepting and loving what you find.

I was sitting in a room with a group of women one evening when one of them said, "I always test men, of course, everybody does." And then she turned to me and asked, "How do you test men, Merle?" I thought for a moment and then said, "I don't think I test men actually. I am always afraid of doing anything that might cause them to go away." And the room laughed as if I'd made a joke. But I knew when I thought about it that what I said was true and what she said was as well. Because to her, whose father had left, men were perfidious, and to me they were wounded because mine died, so she tested and I cossetted and we both called the personalities that resulted "mine."

"I am part of all that I have met," Tennyson wrote, and he no more than we. It is all but impossible to know where we leave off and where another begins, or where the past meets the future, or where our hopes meet our fears, only that another is another and brings all that with them as well.

"I was taught when I was young that if people would only love one another, all would be well with the world," George Bernard Shaw once wrote. "This seemed simple and very nice, but I found, when I tried to put it in practice, not only that other people were seldom lovable, but that I was not very lovable myself," and one would have to agree he had a problem there. And maybe it's a problem most of us have as well. There is something about love that seems to require us to be bigger and better than we are. And rather than live with those who see us as we are, and accept the person whom we see reflected in their eyes, we tell them they could do better themselves or that we are moving on, when what we really want to know is can they love us as we are and can we love ourselves? And will they be patient with us while we're learning and give us credit for trying even when we don't get it right?

I knew a man once who was a graduate student doing a Ph.D. and who lived with a woman whom he loved although they had very little money to celebrate that love, and very little leisure to think in terms of celebration.

The woman, a student as well, and an artist also, loved beautiful things and so the two often spent their weekends in flea markets, chasing down treasures for two and three dollars which they took home and shined up and repaired and repainted, and in this way they created their furnishings, their entertainment, and their shared life.

In time, this couple parted and both went their own ways and the man, now quite successful, married and had a family and the woman, although she didn't marry, made a life for herself as well. And when the man came to the city where she lived, he'd visit and they'd talk together awhile, each telling the other, without quite knowing it, what grew from the life they'd lived.

One day the man asked the woman to help him buy his wife a present for their anniversary and Christmas and her birthday, adding, as if she'd understand, "You know I was never very good about buying presents. I'm a little bit behind."

So they went out shopping together and the man

chose an antique silver tea service and gave it to his wife, because he could never have bought it for the woman who helped him choose it when he wished he could, and she went home to drink her tea from a small brown crockery pot, knowing what he'd done.

There are those who would have thought that what he did was cruel, and others who would have called it lacking in thought, insensitive to a fault, but I think it is more accurate to think of it as an undoing of something he wished he could have done differently once. And as such, the tea service was really a gift he made to himself and not to either woman, a kind of graduation present, a genuflection in his own direction, albeit a developmental lag, and what he wanted to say was, "I would have loved you better if only I'd been able. Please love me as I wish I'd been."

I don't know why we confuse asking another for approval with giving them ours, but it seems more natural for most of us to ask for love than to give it, more satisfying to skate on that shining feeling of being appreciated than to appreciate another ourselves. It is not easy to give up our everlasting negotiations for our own approval, and our spasms of self-doubt, and see another as a separate person, one who could use a little approval themselves. Nor is it simple to understand we are offering what we are, not what we have, so giving our respect and acceptance to another makes us a lover and is the best gift we can give.

Respect is love in plain clothes, someone once said, and so is acceptance and understanding and really being known. And when someone really understands what makes you who you are, they've made a friend for life. And so does someone who values you just the way you are.

There are people who idealize others as a way of solacing themselves, and others who keep you on a treadmill, auditioning for their approval, but always seem to keep the approval strangely in reserve. And there are people who seem to always be in crisis, needing you to continually reassure them, but it's hard to find a person who gives as good as they get or one who loves you for your self.

Donald Barthelme wrote a wonderful story, called "CityLife", about the day God dies and the angels no longer know what to do now that their main function, adoring God, is no longer possible. They called a meeting to try to figure things out.

All the angels assembled: "Angels of Quaking, who surrounded the heavenly throne; Masters of Howling and Lords of Shouting, whose work is Praise; messengers, mediators, watchers, warmers."

They consulted a paper on The Psychology of Angels (written in 1957). Angels, they learned, turned out to be very much like men. They tried to consider their new relation to the cosmos. ("Is an angel more like a quetzal or more like a man? or more like music?") And they lamented that adoring God was no longer possible.

After the lamentation had gone on for hundreds and hundreds of whatever the angels use for time, an angel proposed that lamentation be the function of angels eternally, as adoration was formerly. The mode of lamentation would be silence, in contrast to the unceasing chanting of Glorias that had been their former employment. But it is not in the nature of angels, so the idea of lamentation was discarded as a possible future career move for angels.

There were other suggestions, none overwhelmingly attractive. A famous angel appeared on television. His garments glistened as if with light. He talked about the situation of the angels now. Angels, he said, are like men in some ways. The problem of adoration is felt to be central. The angels, he said, had tried adoring each other, as we do, but had found it finally "not enough." He said they were continuing to search for a new principle.

Amatus interruptus takes many forms. The angel looks for a god to love, the troubadour yearns for the lover, the narcissist longs to be loved himself, but all of them find love never.

"For one human being to love another, that is perhaps the most difficult of all our tasks, the ultimate, that last test and proof, the work for which all other work is but preparation," Rilke wrote, and he was right. It is easy enough to love the one who got away or the one we never got, the real trick is to love ourselves enough to let someone know who we really are, and to pay them the same respect. Time and love, a smart man once said, are two things one can only spend but never buy, and to earn them, one must really try.

5

Singing our own songs

I knew a man once who had lost his wife and was looking for another, some days a little desperately. One day he met a woman who he thought would fit the bill, so he invited her to dinner and told her of his plan. "I am willing to make a big investment," he told her, and she smiled at him but indicated she was not for sale.

He didn't get her message so on their next date he told her what his sister-in-law had found out about her at the hairdresser and added as if it was a joke, "It's always nice to know you're held in high esteem by those who hold sharp objects to your head." And she smiled again but wondered why he'd take a hairdresser's opinion of her, a man he didn't even know, rather than trust his own impressions of her or ask her about herself.

They didn't see each other for a week or so and then he called again. "I've been out of town," he told her, "on some business I had to do. And while I was away I checked up on your marriage. I'm not proud of this you understand," he added apologetically, "but it was important for me to know why your marriage failed and what repercussions that would have for me." "I understand," she said, "but I would have to ask you this. Why is it that you want me, when you don't have a clue who I am? And have you ever asked yourself why I should want you since in the sum total of our three dates what you've proven to me is how little judgment you have and how little you trust yourself."

A lot of us go a-courting thinking we are telling another how much we value them, when what we're really saying is how lucky they are to get us. And what we think is loving is really judging, auditioning, correcting, and rejecting, although we think that it is love.

If you want love you have to give it, and sitting in judgment is the opposite of love. Besides, one person's set of expectations does not a relationship make, because when you have expectations which weren't agreed upon by both, you have a tyranny and a power struggle or a hamster on a treadmill but none of this is love.

Perhaps it is that twisting and turning to get another glimpse of ourselves in the pool, but some part of each of us deceives ourself and confuses our fears and needs with gifts of love. I guess that's why self-love is so often unrequited and why so many who await the discovery of love go companionless and uninvited. And why we often try to colonize another either with our imagination, or with our demands and expectations, without understanding that we are failing to recognize them.

There was a young woman once who was going with a man almost twice her age who had been married a time or two before. He loved her in his fashion, and she loved him in hers, but their relationship was a stormy one and most evenings seemed to end in anger, or as she put it to me once, in a fit or a sulk or a cry. "What seems to be the problem?" I asked, and was told, "He keeps promising that we'll get married but then fails to take steps. And when I find us an apartment he always vetoes it for reasons that are arbitrary and nonsensical, ones he's just made up. And I want to have a baby before it is too late, and he always agrees in principle but that's as far as we seem to get. He's had two children already and I think he's scared. But maybe he's just too selfish and wants us to stay the way we are."

It was hard for me to make her understand that she already had her answer and there was nothing further to discuss. That her terms were not his terms and they didn't have a bargain nor would they, no matter how much she tried to get him to agree and no matter what wiles she thought to use. And harder still to make her understand that she wasn't listening to him any more than he was listening to her. And that the answer didn't lie in trying to manipulate him but in deciding what to do.

We are more anxious to speak than to be heard, more anxious to be heard than to listen. And sometimes even when we hear, we don't take in the message, so intent are we on making our needs known we forget the other has needs as well.

We live in very unromantic times, it is said. Although I am not sure "romantic" is the word that I would use to summon up the courtesies we fail to show each other, the ways we patronize and ignore and render impotent the feelings of the other, as we rush to see ourselves in love's incandescent light.

Parry, finesse, elude. Deflect but don't connect. As if to let others know our feelings for them would be to give them a power over us, as if showing our respect for them would be to give them points when we want all the points ourselves.

Somehow we go from seeing the other as the person who will rescue us from our loneliness to the person who holds us there, from the parent we have to woo to the sibling we have to beat out. And our emotional arteries harden and we don't give them an inch.

I remember a man who'd lived with the same woman for more than ten years, confessing to me that he and his lady got along much better in recent times because he'd finally realized that "all those things she does are not just done to give me a tough time. You know," he said, in a confidential tone, "Evelyn is a very contrary person and I've had to learn to live with that, but I realize now that often when she seems to be just trying to get my goat, she's really doing what she thinks is best. And I've learned to respect that, if not to like it, and if I am not mistaken, she does it less."

I tried to suggest to him that his seeing her as contrary still needed a little work and that what he called contrary, she might call having to shout a little to be heard, but I am not sure he got my point, so intent was he on telling me what it had taken him ten years to learn. That she wasn't out to get him, she was just another human being with thoughts and feelings of her own.

When the United Nations was first formed, they found that people from different countries had different distances which they considered comfortable for each to stand apart from each. So the people from an Eastern country might come right up to talk to a Westerner who would automatically back away, and the Easterner, feeling stranded, would move in on him wondering what it was he'd said.

It is not much different with individuals. We each have a distance which we try to keep, and one man's intimacy is another's invasion, one man's closeness another person's crowd, so while we all say we want love, most of us have a line you must not cross. And many couples are made up of two people who have an agreement, although they may not know it, a contract that guarantees that if one advances the other will retreat, a kind of "who's turn is it to have the headache tonight" understanding, which keeps them both high and dry and safe.

There is a war between the sexes, don't you know, someone is always saying to me, as if that's the way it was and the way it would always be. But I can't help trying to understand, trying to make sense of it, even trying to put an end to it with peaceable means. And while I know this is simplistic, I should like to offer it now. Power is anathema to intimacy, as it is to love, because when you have power, you have fear. So if you are trying to get closer to someone than you are right now, try recognizing their power rather than showing them yours.

Recognize all those push-aways for what they

are, one or the other of you saying, "I am scared. Get off my toes." And instead of giving tit for tat, as if this is a bad thing, or bringing out the assertiveness training to protect your rights, look for a way to show them that they are on firm ground.

When one person withholds respect, either by not giving credit where credit is due or by making it impossible for the other to say what's on their mind, or by ridiculing them or not giving them time or not hearing or not listening or not remembering or not getting it straight, that's the end of that. And that's just as true when one tries to sway the other through manipulating their emotions rather than by understanding what they really feel and why.

Some people make it heavy weather to tell them anything, by yelling or weeping or crying foul, or viewing each thought of the other as a disloyalty to them, but in the end, it's themselves they cheat. Intimacy can't exist with power games. It needs pure air to breathe. And respect isn't respect if it's a one-way street. So both parties must respect each other and both parties must respect themselves, otherwise you don't have intimacy although you might have something else, perhaps a debating society, or an agreement not to meet, but you don't have intimacy, of that I have no doubt.

Intimacy requires accommodation and gentleness at the core, and goes with phrases like, "If it bothers you I won't do it," and "Now I understand." And "Thank you for telling me that. I hadn't seen it in that light." And "I appreciate you taking the time to get through my defenses. I am sorry I put up such a fight."

I know some people would think these phrases wimpish, and feel that if you start to talk like that, you'll be maneuvered into a corner or you'll get taken advantage of, but you'd be surprised how much power there is in respect, and how much respect comes back, and how much more intimacy there is when you empower someone instead of overpower them, and how much more love.

There has been a lot of talk lately about intimacy, and the search for it consumes many, although there seems to be some confusion as to where to look. Some talk of it as if intimacy were synonymous with sex but others disagree, stating that shared feelings are more important than shared bodies and so is the ability to depend, and the freedom to be yourself. And they say that there is no intimacy unless there is mutual acceptance and mutual trust, no matter whatever else there is, and I would side with them.

But what is this psychic space, this common ground we seek to share, called intimacy—this place where you can exist in your own inner light and not be judged, this haven where your vulnerabilities don't humiliate you, where sex is always warm and close and all your funny lines are understood, and there is always someone back to back with you when you take on the world?

It's a place where not only joy can be shared but

hardship too, it's an eye that catches yours across a room, it's not having to look your best, it's knowing someone else so well you can no longer tell where they begin and you leave off, like in the cartoon in which one old person says to another, "Which one of us doesn't like broccoli?"

It's pet names and making plans, a cup of tea brought to bed, seeing life through someone else's eyes, even when they're not there. It's being covered up in the night, having suntan oil applied to your back. It's a hug when you need it and even when you don't, and it's knowing you have a date for Saturday night.

When there is love

A woman I know once told me that when her business failed she became very angry at her husband although she did not know why. And he, no doubt sensing her anger and feeling no longer adored, announced he wanted out of the marriage, although he wasn't able to say why himself. It took them a long time and a lot of sleepless nights, during which they talked until dawn, to figure out what was happening and to find their way back again. "I think," she told me over tea one day, a long time after the event, "that I was mad at him because if he couldn't save the business, he was just as powerless as I and I'd been wrong to think of him as my prince, he was just an ordinary guy. And I think he wanted out because I no longer was a success in his eyes, and only if I was could he go on being the prince, which is the only role he knows."

Who is to say how we fail each other and how we fail ourselves? Only that it is very easy to run into a scrim we put between ourselves and the other, which neither of us can see, made up of expectations and fears about ourselves, which we hope the other will save us from. And that when we do battle with ourselves "we make rhetoric out of our quarrel with ourselves," as Yeats once said, instead of the other way around.

Expectations can make us feel envious, abandoned, fearful, and disappointed and that it is all someone else's fault. And even when they have done nothing we can actually put our finger on, something they haven't done can make us spin around. It's as if the other person stepped on a minefield and tripped off an explosive charge, blowing us both apart, but they look at us as if we did it and we look accusingly at them. And neither of us knows where to start or how to put the pieces back.

There is no edge to expectations, they keep moving, things you don't even know you feel surface and then won't go away. And somehow it's always the other guy who "should have," never really ourselves.

The loved one holds the key to how we feel about ourself. They can say with a flick of the eye that we are desirable or discardable, precious or pathetic. So if we don't feel the way we want, it is their fault and they are the one we blame. Because that's the role we've given them to play.

Our expectations for the ones we love are great—a lot greater than the ones we have for ourselves. Our loved ones carry the burden of how we feel about ourselves, like a monkey on their back. And we, in turn, carry the burden of how they feel about themselves, so if we don't think they are doing a good job of making us happy, they don't feel good about themselves. And if they don't feel good about themselves, it's a no-win for everyone.

In every relationship, there is a hidden contract and part of that contract, although almost always unstated, is to shore up the other person's self-image and make them feel good about themselves. Which is why more than one person has left a marriage saying, "My wife doesn't understand me," when what they really mean is, unfortunately she does. And why a lot of people have exited screaming, "I could never make you happy," when what they really meant is, you would never give me the approval I seek.

There is a story told about Moses Mendelssohn, a Jewish theologian and philosopher of the eighteenth century, about the day he went to meet his bride for the first time. Mendelssohn was a hunchback, and his intended, seeing his deformity from afar, refused to come downstairs to meet him. "Madam," he said, calling up to her, "I will leave if you wish but first please let me tell you something that you should know. It is announced in heaven before a person is to be born who it is they will marry, and who will be strong and who will be weak, who will be beautiful and who will not. And when I heard that my bride-to-be was to have a twisted back, I said, 'No, please! Give that crippled back to me instead of her. I will carry it for her.' And I have worn this hump all these years in your place so that you could be beautiful as I knew you should." And as the story goes, on hearing these words she came down the stairs and became his wife.

I tell you this story now, apocryphal or true, because it has always made me uncomfortable, even as I knew it was meant to be a story about sacrifice and kindness carried to the highest power. And I think what makes me uneasy is the knowledge that this is what we all in a less dramatic way do, when we make our love an albatross for someone else to carry because we don't trust them to love us as we are, so we make them responsible for perfecting us, without considering the cost to them.

I t's hard work to shore up another's self-image when they don't believe in themselves, to have to give back a satisfactory reflection to someone who won't like what they see if they see the real thing. And even harder to love somebody who can't love you because they can't love themselves. But the hardest thing of all is to be blamed for not accomplishing the impossible, and abandoned as a failure and a cheat, when the only cheating that went on was their cheating themselves.

If we don't let others love the person that we are, but ask them to pretend we are something we wish ourselves to be, we are saying, before they get a chance, that we aren't lovable, and what's more, that we don't trust them. And that we'd rather continue to take the cheap bait than to know ourselves or them.

And we are saying as loud as we can say it that we don't value this person, whom we profess to love, for the person that they are, only as a set of services and an apparatus for making ourselves look good so we can love ourselves, but we are not saying we love them and, in fact, we don't.

It is easy to confuse wanting to like yourself with liking or not liking someone else but they are not the same. When you like someone, you like them for the qualities that are intrinsic to them. And when you like them only because they help you stroke yourself, the only qualities you care about are the ones that reflect positively on you. So you might even prefer them to have qualities that aren't too likable, if this makes you look better than you otherwise would.

A woman once told me of marrying a man who was raising a daughter all by himself, who claimed to want and need her help. But as time went on, she could see he found it difficult to share the daughter's affection with anyone else, and while he talked of wanting the woman he married to help him parent this child, the truth was the view of himself as the martyr father was more precious than giving his child a mother or having a partner in life.

"I tried as hard as I could," she told me some time after she'd left, "but he actually blocked any moves I made toward the child, and then blamed me for not trying hard enough. And I couldn't live with the view of myself as the wicked stepmother so that he could believe himself better than good. And I knew he'd never really let me in because to let the world see how helpful I'd been would be to cost him the superman role he'd built for himself."

We can all talk of give and take, of what one must do if one wants love, of all the sacrifices one must make, but the hardest thing of all is to see other persons as they really are, and love them for themselves, and understand that hearts cannot be demanded as a tithe, they must be understood. And one does not earn a lover's wage by giving love to oneself, only by giving it to another.

I am sure if I asked the man who could not share his daughter's love what happened to his second wife he would say she didn't love him enough and that he tried his best, and that his little daughter had to have first dibs, and he must do without, but I would say it's sometimes hard to love someone for their loyalty, their kindness, and their courage when their good qualities rival your own, and many of us who say we want to be loved, ask really to be admired.

A lot of men have borrowed me to massage themselves and I have borrowed some, but rarely did I find a man who really cared to find out who it is I am. "Man is in love and loves what vanishes" is what Yeats said, but I say, that's not the case, love goes nowhere. It is always there. It's just we confuse it with our needs and put false gods in its place.

It's not easy to know when one gives love and when one asks for it, where one person's ego starts and another's ends, when another's need is greater than yours, and yet these are questions one must ask if one wants to talk of love. Because often when we think we are saying, "These are my jewels," as we lay them at another's feet, what they are hearing is, "This is a stick-up. Hand over yours!" Which is why, of course, they retreat.

"On the far side of the subjective, on this side of the objective, on the narrow ridge where I and thou meet, there is the between," Martin Buber wrote. Could anyone put it better than that? How narrow is that ridge, that sacred ground, where we mutually beget each other, and all the love we give away keeps coming back again! It gets narrower all the time.

One can make deals, or one can make love, of this make what you will. A deal asks back and love gives away and a contract has to be paid. But love never comes due, because once given away, it always comes back to you.

Part Three

BETWEEN

7

Looking out for love

What is this territory we share—"the between," as Martin Buber called it? In social terms it is the family, immediate and extended, including children joint and sometimes blended, in-laws, out-laws, friends, and hangers-on. All those one acquires and inherits. It is a world based on bloodlines and bank accounts and occasions and celebrations.

In physical terms, it is the domestic plant—the world of kitchen, bathroom, and bedroom—a world that dispenses comforts and requires reciprocity. It is a world of food and sex and clean laundry.

In emotional terms, it is that joint persona—that "Us"—which is neither you nor them, but is somehow different and something more than both of you put together. It is that thing called "The Relationship" which permits you to be in private together, and to be embarrassed for each other, and proud of each other, and causes people to think of you as one entity instead of two. It is a world of hopes and fears and joys and tears.

"Chains do not hold a marriage together," Simone Signoret once said. "It is threads, hundreds of tiny threads, which sew people together through the years," and she was right of course: threads of many colors and hues woven more tightly with the years, threads for secrets shared and promises kept, threads of obstacles overcome and compromises found, of shoulders leaned on and ears that listened, of hands that reached out and hearts that met, and sometimes cracked, and broke, and mended.

There is a lovely scene I remember from a short story I read years ago, about an older couple who are out for a stroll on a summer's night and they pass a house where they once lived, now in the process of being renovated. Through the open door they can see the wallpaper in the hall stripped off to reveal several layers below.

"Oh! Remember the rose wallpaper?" she asks him. "I think it was up when you had your affair with Eva," she adds as if talking of something that happened to others.

"Was that when you were in the hospital?" he

asks, adding, "When you were sick for all those months after the baby?" "I think it was the same year," she agrees and then adds, "Sometimes I wonder how we made it through." And then they link arms again and stroll off again together.

Who is to say what makes some marriages survive and others fail? Is it strengths or fears, is it commitment to the idea of marriage or to the marriage itself, is it a belief in the other or a belief in oneself? And what part love, and is love enough? Certainly one of the largest causes of divorce is divorce itself.

Few of us know what caused our own marriage to last or leave, let alone any other, just that it's getting harder every day to believe in "the between" as a place where you can run to and be safe. And Ralph Lauren's making millions out of everyone's broken dreams of hearth and home and country weekends.

The caller and the called was how Buber described it, speaking of a reciprocal relationship in which the participants were so symbiotic that, like dancers, one always stepped backward when the other stepped forward, and no one ever tripped the other up. But they are harder to find these days, those relationships. Feminism, which brought us many good things in the last decade or so, among them more flexibility of roles, has also, in smudging the boundaries between the sexual roles, made it harder for one to know where one might legitimately say, "I deserve your respect because I am doing my job." Now both sexes feel guilty about twice as much. Men do not any longer just have to worry about not supporting their families, they have to worry about learning to cook as well, and women, who once had only to worry about being a good wife and mother, now have to worry about climbing the career ladder too. What's more, women's liberation has taught us all a valuable lesson about the many hinges on which self-esteem hangs.

I knew a woman once who had a career as an advertising executive and a whole life of her own which she gave up to marry a man who wanted her to play mother to his four kids. She'd had a career for a considerable time at this juncture, but she'd never been a wife or mother so she made her decision joyously and never looked back. But one day I heard her say, making a gift of necessity as lovers often do, that she considered herself lucky that her husband always gave her the housekeeping money and never asked where it went. And I heard myself answer, with more vehemence than I'd realized I felt, "The two of you have a partnership, a business called a marriage, and it has several pieces of work it must do. Run the plant, raise the children, look after the sick and dying, make the money, and plan the leisure. And you do four of them and he does one, so I don't think you need feel grateful, because had you stayed in your job instead of agreeing to help him be a better father and son, and a better businessman, you'd have a lot more clout today and he'd have a lot less cash and a lot less pride in himself."

And she answered me so sadly I can still hear her voice. "I am glad you said that. I lose sight of it a lot of the time. In this world, which thinks women must do everything and do it all at once but then tallies up the money made and only allots points for that, it's sometimes hard for me to respect myself, a lot harder than when I had a job. But the part that hurts the most is that my husband doesn't always understand the contributions that I've made, and it's his respect I want!"

My mother used to say you had to give more than fifty percent if you wanted to have a good relationship, and no one would disagree with that, but if you are called upon to feed your partner's good impression of himself with your own, can that be the right fifty percent to give? Or is the trick to give yourself full value for the gifts you make, so you don't require it back from someone else? Maybe the real work is to learn to give from a good place, so your self-respect grows with every gift, and so does that of the one to whom you make the gift.

I only know, though hard be the task—this business of "becoming" we call finding love—and too easy the opportunity to become convex to another's concave, to become the limits of ourselves and hold the other responsible. And only too comfortable our tendency to make and mould the other out of things past, instead of really coming to understand the mystery of the beloved. Still we need and want each other's love, and must find ways to share it, if we are to become the people we were meant to be and help the ones we love become more themselves.

It used to be thought that being alone was frightening and if one could just find somebody with whom to share one's life, everything would be fine, but more and more today, "The Between" is recognized as the real battlefield, the arena in which the real compromises must be made, the forum in which we negotiate our vulnerability, the place where we come hoping to be made whole, and in which, ironically, we cast each other in the narrowest roles.

Many marriages have washed up on the shoals of change in the last twenty years, my own included, victims of transitions not well negotiated. Mine seemed to work well enough when my husband was a law student and I a social worker. But when he graduated and the baby came and I was supposed to metamorphose out of the energetic girl who had worked while he went to law school, sprinting between the social work agency and the graduate school, sometimes twice over in a day, and become the stay-at-home mom who polished little white boots and made peanut butter cookies, I failed the test. He thought that was our deal and he was right, but I still couldn't do it. I was having an identity crisis with no job to define me, recognized and applauded in the outside world. I knew the world that claimed a woman's place was in the home then discounted her. I thought if he really loved me he'd be able to see that. And wouldn't want that for me. Wouldn't view my life as an adjunct to his, to be made over each decade to suit his latest requirements, but as a life of equal value. He thought he'd married a misfit. And wondered why, if I didn't want to do the work, I had applied for the job.

So the marriage died, and since the participants thrived one could argue one should let sleeping dogs lie, but I should like to say this. I thought for some many years after my marriage ended that my husband and I had separated because we hadn't agreed on what style of marriage we wanted, but I don't see it that way any more. Today if you asked me, I'd likely tell you it had a lot more to do with our not being able to figure out how to share the respect. Maybe if I'd understood that my husband, just out of law school, had a lot invested in proving he could support his wife and infant son, I'd have seen him less as an oppressor, more as a fellow navigator on a stormy sea of change. Maybe if I had found a way to give him my respect, he'd have found a way to understand I needed his. Maybe if we'd each had more respect for ourselves we'd have needed less from each other.

It's been a long time since women going out to work was the hot issue but each decade brings new changes to adjust to, and couples who hope to make it for the long haul have to learn to traverse them all.

There are many people walking away from marriages these days saying, "That's not my dream any more," and issues of loss and growth fill the magazines and TV screens. Sometimes one wonders if trying to wrest happiness from coupledom isn't about as easy as trying to crack a combination safe without the combination, but no relationship thrives that doesn't have enough self-respect to go around and those in which the individuals have to fight for it between themselves like dogs for a bone aren't likely to make it, no matter what else they do.

The truth is giving and getting help in negotiating the growth of our self-respect, our becoming, if you will, is the only reason to be together these days. There was a time when we needed each other for support, both financial and domestic, but each sex can do those things pretty well for themselves today. Emotional support is the only thing we really need each other for now. And if we aren't able to do that for each other, there won't be any reason to be together at all.

There is more to that story about that marriage of mine made and played out a million light years ago in the dawn of the Betty Friedan years. And if I am to tell you true, I must tell you all. When the world had changed a little bit, and my husband had tried out his legal feet, he came back to me and said, "I was wrong. I didn't understand. You were ahead of your time."

And if the truth be told, it is only fair to say, I didn't respond in kind. I thanked him for that acknowledgment and the generosity it took, but told him that it didn't change things for me. It wasn't for me any better to have love offered because I was in favor, any more than it had been to have it withdrawn because I was not. And somewhere deep inside of me I knew I needed to find someone to love who would value me whether I was in or out.

One of the ironies that confronts you as you get older is that you find it wasn't so much that you didn't have the right answers when you were younger as that you didn't have the right questions and that's what made the answers wrong. What is it that they say about all of us growing too soon old and too late smart? But I am certain of one thing and I can tell you that. No one wins who just saves himself. And if it's love, it doesn't ask you to make that choice.

8

Two cheers for equality

There was a little old lady living next door to me when I was a young bride, a woman of some considerable intelligence who, although then in her eighties, lived alone in an elegant apartment and spent her days reading books she hadn't had time for when she was young. She was waiting in the hall for my husband well after midnight the night our son was born and she rode in the ambulance to the hospital when another tenant on our floor had a heart attack. She was everybody's family and we were hers. When my marriage started to come apart at the seams she brought me a book. It was the story of Lilith, Adam's first wife, the one before Eve. Lilith was willful, I learned from the book jacket, so God recalled her and made a new mate for Adam out of his own rib so that she would be a helpmate to him and not a separate person with ideas of her own.

That was enough for me. I never read the book. I considered the idea of self-sacrifice for women to be obsolete. I believed in equality, in respect, and in choice. And most of all, I believed in love and thought that anything that stood between me and happiness couldn't be love at all.

I didn't know yet that equality means standing alone, and does not allow for interconnectedness. Or that seeking respect in the world we lived in then meant playing by men's rules. I did not know that there was a delicate balance between feeling protective and feeling responsible and that, if you disturb it, you can trade away the love you have for the respect you seek. Or that when you don't feel needed, you don't feel loved and when you don't feel loved, you don't feel safe. Or that any of this had to do with fidelity and trust. I just took my chances and exercised my choices and in the process I discovered a lot of what my wise old neighbor was likely trying to tell me once long ago.

Anne Morrow Lindbergh said, "A good relationship has a pattern like a dance and it is built on some of the same rules. The partners do not need to hold tightly because they move confidently in the same pattern, intricate but gay and swift and free, like a country dance of Mozart's.

To touch heavily would be to arrest the pattern and freeze the movement, to check the endlessly changing beauty of its unfolding. Now arm in arm, now face to face, now back to back, it does not matter which. Because they know they are partners moving to the same rhythm, creating a pattern together, and being invisibly nourished by it." But she wrote about an earlier time. The patterns are all shattered now and the rules are made and broken every day anew. What once seemed exciting and freeing now seems confusing and chaotic. And many people wish they knew exactly what steps to take.

Women used to define themselves by the care they took of others but, in a world that admired those who went to the moon rather than those who stayed at home, most of them gave that up. And nourishing, always low on the pay scale, got classed as a second-class art. And women who practiced it started to feel ashamed of themselves, as if they had somehow failed to meet the mark.

The title housewife one had accepted with simple pride now took on the prefix "justa" as if it never came plain and women who still answered to it apologized for living and the men who loved them took their clean socks out of the drawer and felt they were shortchanged.

Female pride, now like men's, had to do with showing you had what it takes, beating the other guy out, getting the promotion, and not letting down the team. And a world that used to look down on women started to take them seriously at last, although family dinners became a luxury and so did homemade pies.

Women began to devalue anything that had to do with their biology because it made them different from men, so no one admitted to having a period any more, and having children became déclassée.

It now became insulting to suggest that a woman couldn't do anything a man could, and one could be called a chauvinist just for opening a door, but men who wanted to show that they were liberated just let a woman support them and that took care of them.

Men do dishes now and take their own shirts in. And a lot of them have learned gourmet cooking, but most toilet bowls go uncleaned. And women are still supposed to advance their husband's career, but nobody is supposed to advance hers and both spouses complain they could use a wife but she has to pay someone to be hers.

Although there isn't universal legislation yet to pay women the same as men. But nobody seems to mind if they work twice as long. And men who leave the office early to pick up a child get points today but a woman still gets fired.

Women jumped into the male sexual ethos too, with an assist from the pill, feeling so unfettered, generous, and brave, happy to slough off the immorality of bartering sex for love, and the discomfort of the old interaction which pushed them against their own natures and made it a crime to love. And like the little boy who was warned that masturbation made you blind, they kept doing it a long time after they needed glasses, and found it hard to give it up, even after they found that the old "If he wins, she loses" number was gone and the "If they win, she still loses" number was in its place.

Sexually, women are free now, no more chattels and man's possession. Virginity isn't a value any more to be traded and made a bride's price. Women have orgasms now and sexual needs, although when it comes to the effect of contraceptives and abortions on the body the woman still always pays. And it can be a little tiresome to have to explain that being liberated doesn't mean you sleep with everyone, but that you sleep with whom you choose. And some days it is annoying to be considered always available to anyone at all.

Maybe it was the loss of courtship, maybe it was that procreation now became recreation and the forbidden became de rigueur. I just know we lost something important when sex stopped being ladies first and became every man for himself. And women who thought sexual freedom would lead to romance and love have had to think again.

It's been a hard time for women lately with the job of career added to the duties of mother and wife and only too often the job of breadwinner too. And many of them who entered the work force because they were sick of being treated like children didn't like it any better when they got treated like supermom.

Still there have been a lot of gains for women in

the last several years. We get to have our own money now, and to develop our potential as we decide we will, and no one has to have a family today unless they choose to and these were all worth fighting for, and I'm glad we did. But the gains have all been in the rational world and not in the emotional world at all, as if women joined men in doing their work but no one is minding our store. And a lot of things we cared about and care about still are falling by the wayside while we scramble to look after number one. And lot of the things which fed on each other before feed on themselves today.

It is galling to be lined up with those who say, "You have come a long way, baby, but is this the right road? And is it going where you thought it was?" Or even worse those who say, "So you thought it would be easy, what a baby you are! Don't you know Rome wasn't built in just one day!" And I could lay loose in a place of shadows, soldier on in silence and keep my opinions to myself. But as that has never been my way, let me share my confusions with you instead.

What we were looking for in the search for the dignity of women was simply a chance to feel good about ourselves. Why should we have had to pay so much for that? And if this all adds up to a discouraging message, who is there to blame? I only know we've forfeited protection for equality, plundered nurturing for self-development, squandered courtship and loyalty for sexual freedom, laid waste family life with ambition, and self-respect for everyone is further away than ever before.

"Very early in life I knew that the only object in life was to grow," someone said to me proudly the other day and I would, of course, concur. But where is it written that one only grows alone? Or that the time spent in the service of others keeps one from one's goals? Carl Jung was once asked by a student what was the shortest route to achieve his chosen end, and he replied, "The detour," and then added, "of that there is no doubt."

We've been doubting it a lot lately trying to get there faster, flying now and paying later, trying to reach that place called happiness, certain we can do it quicker than our parents' generation, even though we can't find it on any map. Throwing out the rule book and the family Bible, so intent are we on finding love.

There is an old religious poem I can't quite remember which goes something like this. "The food that I share with others/Is the food that nourishes me. The strength that I spend for others/Is the strength that I retain. The freedom I seek for others Shall take away my pain. The load that I lift in others Is the path God walks with me." I wish I knew who wrote it but I don't. Sorry to say.

"Things that I longed for in vain and things that I got, let them pass. Let me truly possess the things that I spurned and overlooked," a friend once said to me. Could he have been right? I just know that I was judged a misfit in the sixties, and a trailblazer in the seventies, but for me there is no change. Because I am still asked to pay with one part of myself for another, to foreclose on my heart to buy out my brain.

"We receive but what we give," Coleridge said, there is no other way. So cherishing others must be given the respect it deserves. And men must learn that lesson and women must learn it back and all of us who think we know it must practice just the same. There are a lot of what used to be called female values that both sexes must hurry to reclaim and narcissism must be renounced by both as the empty state that it is.

The Greeks have a myth about the beautiful young goddess called Persephone who, seeing some beautiful narcissus one day, reaches for them and is pulled into the underworld by Hades, the god of the nether regions, who has put the pretty flowers there to tempt her.

Her mother, Demeter, goddess of summer, bargains with Hades for her safe return and he finally agrees if Persephone returns to the underworld for half of each year. Which is why the earth flowers for only half a year when the goddess of spring returns, the myth tells us, but it also tells us that narcissism kills, and that what makes the earth flower and bloom again is the caring of one by another.

9

Tearing down paradise, putting up a parking lot

There was a funny scene in Nora Ephron's auto-biographical novel, *Heartburn*, when the heroine and her unfaithful husband have reconciled and are flying back for another try at marriage, she larger than life with their second child and clutching their balky toddler. The stewardess comes down the aisle of the shuttle to collect the fare, and she hands over her VISA card, somehow understanding even at this moment that she isn't in a marriage, she is on a dutch date.

It made me laugh when I read it but it made me cry too. There have been moments like that in my own life as well. I can remember arguing with a man with whom I shared my life once, a man who had sharpened his wits studying logic, about the ways we might divide our expenses. "Let's just divide them down the middle," he argued. "It's the easiest." "Even in restaurants?" I whined, feeling unliberated and more than a little silly. "Sure, why not?" he countered. "What's wrong with that?" "Nothing," I said, "I guess. Except that it makes no allowance for hospitality, or generosity, or celebration, or giving, and without those things there would be no reason for us to eat together."

He had logic and I had feelings, but it was his world I was living in now. And I was the new boy trying to prove I had what it takes to get admitted to the big leagues.

When the pill liberated conception from companionship for the first time since the dawn of time, it created for the baby boomer generation the longest adolescence in history—a kind of summer life sans responsibilities at an age when their parents at the same stage were buying into the culture with hard work, ever mindful of the fact that sex had consequences.

For sixties kids it was a new world. Women postponed their families and leapt from the kitchen into the work force, freeing men from the responsibilities of supporting them. Sexual freedom, once the guilty pleasure of men and bad women only, now became the favorite indoor sport of everyone, trivializing both sex and love. Fidelity became a thing of the past, adulthood was thought old-fashioned, responsibility got reclassified as guilt, and those who stayed in a relationship in which they weren't one hundred percent happy were considered to be lacking in imagination, morally reprehensible, strange, or all of the above.

The female liberation movement grew up and a great deal of hope was placed on it to bring about a balance of power between the sexes, and by so doing end the war of the sexes, thought to be caused by men's resentment at women's dependency and women's resentment at men's control, but the divorce rate skyrocketed. And women who once took their new boyfriend home to meet their fathers took him to meet their shrink instead. That condition called marriage that some used to think of as limiting, others as steadying, in which one was protected by a kind of squatter's rights of the heart, was never to be the same again.

In the last twenty-five years, there has been a steady erosion of the bonds between husband and wife, parent and child, citizen and state, employer and employee. And many of us have been sidelined by violations of trust so commonplace we can hardly find a friend to listen to us when we need to vent.

One by one, all the supports for the family have been eroded, like public opinion, and religion, and difficult divorce. We've exchanged it all to worship the god of romantic love, so everything hinges on sexual attractiveness now and men as well as women have become geishas, terrified of being the odd man out in the next game of musical chairs. And because passion, once thought of as a some-time thing, has become a moral right, all of us have become beggars running in the streets, second-hand men all fraying and unravelling.

Whatever permitted those fifties brides to step off their parents' front porch into marriage, with their eyes shining and their grooms to engrave wedding rings with words like, "My everlasting love from this day forth," it doesn't exist today. For better and for worse went too, along with trust.

The contract between men and women is entire-ly different now. Nobody promises to love, honor, and obey any more. At best, they promise to give it their best shot. In a society in which fear of commitment has reached epidemic proportions, marriage is considered the last of the romantic gestures. A triumph of hope over experience, and most people prefer to live together making bargains rather than promises.

It's been popular in the last couple of decades to think of sex as divorced from feelings, as if we were not our bodies, just tenants residing therein, so it was supposed our bodies could slip off with another but we remain un-touched. And people who believed that often went back and forth to the divorce court the way a tongue returns to a sore tooth time and time again, just to see if it still hurts and finds that, in fact, it does.

"It's a man's world," my mother used to say. I can remember arguing with her when she said it. "All that's going to change!" I'd say, and it did. But not the way I hoped. Liberation failed to keep its promises and the biggest surprise of all was that sexaul freedom didn't work for men any better than it did for women.

Availability dulled male appetites, making men fear for their potency, and, dare I say it? having to confront for the first time the fact that their eyes were bigger than their you-know-whats was hard on their egos. There were further humiliations too, like comparisons, and instructions, and rejections, even vibrators, which made the role of sex object, once every male's fantasy, now seem more like a nightmare instead, and somehow Playboy Clubs were going bankrupt all over the land.

As for women, women's lib had hoped to keep them from being abused but it was not successful. The only change in the sexual arena so far has been that now women are abused but with their own permission. Or, as Janis Joplin said in song, "Freedom's just another word for nothing left to lose."

"I've spent up to my emotional income," someone said to me the other day, putting as well as it can be put what Mary McCarthy meant when she said, "In love, as in politics, anarchy is not for the weak." Somehow we've all ended up in a B movie, and life is for many a disease in which they are either in the crisis stage or the convalescence stage but they are never really well.

We have sex as a defiance now, and a duty, as a sport and a sparring, as a power and a performance, as a commodity and a convenience, even as a bargaining chip and a gourmet experience, as a purification rite and a parlor game, but we've lost sight of sex as an intermingling of selves, as an overflowing of one person into another, as an occasion when the blessings of the body are conferred from one to the other as in a benediction. We've sacrificed transcendence to the hope of continual tumescence, which is why we speak of having sex instead of making love.

Perhaps women made a mistake on the way to liberation in thinking that what they wanted was what men had. It's not a surprising mistake when you think of it. Blacks on their way to liberation delayed for a while, envying whites, before they felt confident enough in who they themselves were to ask what they really wanted and to go for that. And women are beginning to do that too.

There was such a lot of self-hate in the early stages of feminism. Why were we so quick to accept men's view of themselves as the only game in town? Why were we so willing to trade in our own magicality for a crack at the corporate ladder? Why did we think we wanted abortions instead of recognizing that what we really wanted was the opportunity to have our babies in loving, committed relationships? Why were we so anxious to show we could be as good as any man, instead of trying to be as good as a woman? Why didn't we hire a public relations consultant to sell the world on female values instead of selling out?

There is so much I need to say, but are there so many who wish to hear? It isn't progress when women define themselves as men, any more than it was progress when they defined themselves against them. As long as women define themselves by men's standards and not by their own, they remain the "Uncola" of the sexes and the world is still deprived. And while I know I leave myself open to a charge of female chauvinism when I say this, I will risk it because we need two sexes in this world and women who attain power in a man's world but have to sacrifice love and children to do it are in the same position as the ancient amazons who cut off their right breasts so that they could hunt with bows and arrows like men. Which is to say the price is a whole lot too high. And not just for women, for men and children too.

I was at a banquet once at a table of strangers except for one couple I knew very well, when the woman of this couple, a free spirit who always spoke her mind, said something one of the other men considered unacceptable. "Alan," he said to her husband, "will you please take responsibility for your wife." "Alan," she snorted back at him, before her husband could answer. "What's this got to do with Alan? How dare you men think you can take a woman's responsibility away from her? And divvy it up between you? If you have anything to say, say it to me directly."

I tell this story now because her retort seemed so right at the time, so brave and true, so swift in its redressing of the wrong. The man, so antediluvian, so patriarchal and self-important. Nor would I do otherwise today, but, and it's just a but, I hope I'd have a little more awareness of what it means for women to cast off men's sense of responsibility for them, a little more respect for the thing I threw away. Because when we unpacked the past and threw away responsibility, with it went a lot of things we should have known we'd need.

Habits of the heart change slowly and when I take my own personal inventory I'd have to say I would never trade the autonomy I have for the protection of some man, but why did I have to trade? Why couldn't we have it all? Why couldn't I have both the right to protect and be protected? Why must one be weak in order for another to feel strong? What is gained if we trade a world in which men are parents and women are children for one in which the positions are reversed? Couldn't we take responsibility for each other, couldn't we give each other care?

The ancient Hasidic Jews used to make sure they wore nothing around their necks while praying so that there would be no break between the heart and the brain. Perhaps we should do the same, because a coordinated heart and mind is what we all must seek. And if I were a praying woman, and there are days I am, I would pray for a new contract between men and women, one that would bring back loyalty and trust. And I would pray for enough self-respect for everyone so that they could give as much love as they seek. So this narrow ridge called "the between" could be mended, and mended with its own thread. Because we have to protect it so that it can protect us.

Part Four

COMMITMENT

10

With dreams come responsibilities

I talked one day with an old boyfriend of mine, a former flambeau, one of my friends would have called him, somebody I couldn't live with and I couldn't live without. He'd been married since I'd seen him last and now was the father of two small boys. "Are you happy?" I asked him. For a moment he scowled at me, and then he said, "What does happy mean? You know that isn't my terminology. In fact, that was what was wrong with our relationship. We had no other reason to be together except that we make each other happy. Happiness has nothing to do with my marriage. My wife and I are involved in a mutual child-raising endeavor, so we can see each day what has been achieved. If that makes us happy, and it often does, well and good. But happiness is not our goal."

I've thought long and hard about what he said that day, and I have to say I think he was right. However unromantic his view, and unromantic is exactly what it was, he was on the right track. Something has gone missing out of love ever since we made it responsible for happiness, sort of like what went missing when freeways replaced country roads and got you there more quickly but cost you the sights and sounds along the way and you arrived with three hours to spare but with your spirit robbed.

Somehow in our hurry we've lost sight of what our grandparents knew before us, that that strange amalgam we call happiness is in a large part pleasure in our own efforts and when we expect happiness rather than produce it, we lose out on the sweat equity which makes us valuable to ourselves and others valuable to us. And we reduce ourselves to our expectations and reduce the other person too. With the result that all we get out of that kind of enterprise is a few loss leaders but real happiness usually stays away.

Perhaps it happened when we started thinking that love should save you from feeling old, or bored, or frightened. Or when we started thinking a little fancy dancing was all that was needed to get you out of a situation that didn't work into one that did. Or when we decided that the "more" we wanted was out there somewhere and not inside ourselves.

Or maybe it began with a belief in destiny, the "this is bigger than both of us" feeling that makes people believe in romantic love, not realizing it is a trick that they play on themselves. Or even earlier, when we first realized we were wounded and needed love to survive. I just know it hasn't been fashionable lately to talk of looking after or of standing by someone else. Perhaps because it smacks of that old word responsibility, once a concept people embraced eagerly, now a word that summons up traps and expectations. And in an age hell bent on happiness that all sounds like something to avoid. So a lot of people keep a bag packed for the big love who might yet come along.

I was sitting in a restaurant recently near a group of people who were talking about a man they all knew who had a wife, and three children, one of them disabled in some way, and his wife had a career and he had a career, and he had fallen in love. "Donald," one of the people at the table remarked, "has never really decided what to do with his life." "That's too bad," another added, "considering that his choice has already been made."

Some people go on changing delusions like costumes all through their lives, looking for the perfect stranger who can help them find their self-respect, never learning that they are their choices and that without commitment no one really has a name. Or that happiness is a by-product, not something someone can hand you, or bring in on a plate.

When we think of for better and for worse, we always think in terms of sickness or of being poor, not of falling out of love or losing your way back to where you were. And we rarely think of not liking "us" and blaming it on them, or them not liking them and blaming it on "us," but that happens a lot today. And often with disastrous results.

The fact is the nuclear family has nothing to blow the pressure when things get a little hot, the way those big families did when there was always a cousin to go fishing with or an aunt to dry your tears. Everything is dependent on the couple now, and on that thing called love. So happiness is just as scarce today, some say scarcer, than it ever was.

The fifties believed in responsibility and commitment and the sixties in freedom and personal growth. And it took most of us all of the seventies to realize you can't have one without the other, and that in fact we need them both. Freedom isn't any good without commitment, and responsibility is what causes personal growth. And the person we hope will help us find a way to love ourself isn't an obstacle to what we want. They're trying to find a way to love themselves as well.

This has been the decade that believed in all or nothing. Making it work hasn't been our thing. We thought seeing a marriage through the tough spots smacked of martyrdom, and living without passion, of water in the veins. We believed in the imperative of the moment, and in what felt good. We thought "duty" was a dirty word, and "hanging in" sucked, so we exchanged them both for keeping an eye out for the main chance and letting it all hang out.

We believed that perfect was somewhere, usually somewhere else. We thought if you loved something, you let it go, not that you cherished it, and we let go of a lot. But the center didn't hold for us. And neither did our dreams and a lot of us learned, to our regret, that there can't be my needs and *your* needs, only *our* needs, if you want to get them met.

"Tough times don't last," says the sign upon my desk, "but tough people do." I filched the sign from a company president's desk. Told him my needs were greater than his. I don't think he quite understood me. Maybe this book will explain. It's funny that those of us who fancy ourselves tough guys in the workplace often think it's okay to cave in pretty quickly when things get tough at home.

I have great admiration for people who understand that honor and reliability and loyalty are not cheap goods to cast aside. People who do what they can with what they have and where they are. People with staying power. People who make things grow. People who understand that it isn't a choice when you promise for better and for worse, but a little of both.

I am not advocating martyrdom, or masochism either, just hanging tough emotionally and having enough self-respect to hold your own with another so both become better. And enough self-love so you don't chase after it all your life, and when there isn't much love coming to you from others you can give some away to them.

What we really want from each other is permission to love ourself, so we can hold our head up under the stars. So we have to learn how to give that permission to others, before we can hope to get. And we have to learn to be kind to each other, and especially kind to ourselves.

Aristotle said, "A friend is another self," and he was right about that. When we really love we treat the one we love like ourself. And we know as we are imperfect so, quite likely, are they. But we keep our faith in ourself and our choice. And if we are having a little trouble loving ourself from time to time, we know we can't blame them.

It would be nice, of course, if we could simply wave a magic wand and the perfect person would appear, and we would become more perfect just by standing near, but it doesn't work that way, and if it's a good impression of yourself you are after, one set of problems is like any other, so changing mates isn't the way to go. What works is giving yourself your own approval, and then giving yours to someone else. Not selling, giving, with no strings attached.

There are people who think that approval should be rationed, so they keep it to themselves, and they don't like to do for others till others do for them. But the trouble is love has a way of tiptoeing up behind you only when you start sharing it with someone else. And because investment plus love often equals happiness, if you disappear every time the going gets tough, or measure out meanly your contribution against someone else's, you become a beggar and a trader instead of a giver, and responsibility becomes a duty, not a calling, and with it goes the magic and the delight.

I remember once asking a nun, as part of an interview I was doing, if she had ever regretted not having children and she answered without hesitating, "Oh yes, I have, of course." And I, rather dismayed at the truth I'd forced out of her and perhaps the resulting pain, hesitated to ask the obvious question, "Do you ever wish you'd not become a nun?" But when I asked it she answered it with the same honesty that she'd answered the first. "No," she said quietly, "No, never. Everything is a choice."

I tell you this story now because I remember how surprising her reply seemed to me then. Astonishing, because she accepted her regret as part of the package, and didn't feel she should either hide it or change things, just accept it as part of the choice that she'd made. Not a sand grain to make a pearl of, or an obstacle to overcome, just a set of problems she'd taken on along with the joys.

"Saddle your dreams before you ride 'em," Mary Webb the English novelist once said, and I would say it too, because with dreams come responsibilities and that's the way it's meant to be. In the end one isn't judged nor does one judge oneself by the things one would have done if one could have, just by the things one did. And those who think they can get to love more quickly without encumbrances generally lose their way.

I knew a man once who almost left his second wife for a beautiful actress with whom he had fallen in love. He'd asked his wife for a divorce before in their long marriage and she'd always said "no" but this time when he asked her she agreed and he, filled with joy and trepidation, ran off to see his lawyer to prepare for his new life. "I guess your wife must have somebody too," the lawyer chanced to remark and the man, much to his surprise, felt his heart lurch. He left his lawyer's office growing steadily more irate. By the time he reached the place where he worked he was beside himself and, unable to contain himself any longer, he streaked across town to his wife's workplace and stormed past her desk into the office of her boss where he grabbed the unsuspecting man by the collar and demanded he tell him the truth. It was several minutes before his wife had him out of the building and back in the car and several minutes more before he realized he had his wife back, and that appeared to be what he sought.

He told me that story a year or so later, the two of us sitting in coats on a winter beach, and he laughed at his own behavior, the tears running down his cheeks. "Are you glad now?", I asked him, "or are you sorry?" "No," he said, "it's probably all for the best. Besides they don't give you a stag if you marry for the third time, so what did I really lose?" Then he gave me his hand and pulled me up and said, "Come on, it's getting late."

There is an Indian folktale about a young brave who went to the village shaman. The boy was troubled and said to the elder, "Help me. There is a war inside my heart. Part of me wants to travel east and another part wants to travel west. What do I do?"

The old man nodded. The boy's problem was a familiar one. "Within each man," the shaman said, "lives two dogs. Both dogs are strong and fight for the man's heart, one to go east, and one to go west. The man chooses which dog will win by deciding which dog he will feed."

I like to think that the man who got his wife back understood that we all must confront the runner in ourselves, if the words "trust yourself to me" are to have any meaning, that he understood when he chose whom he would feed, that in choosing he was deciding who it was he wanted to be.

"Marriage is our last best chance to grow up," Joseph Barth said, and I suspect that is what the man who got back his wife meant when he told me the story of his life. I think he knew he wouldn't have too many chances after this one so he better grab this while he could.

Happiness does not consist of getting everything you want but of wanting everything you have and, while it may seem difficult to imagine making yourself happy on a diet of responsibility and care, it can be done and has.

Joshua Reynolds, the artist, wrote a book of discourses in which he said, "The travellers into the east tell us that when the ignorant inhabitants are asked concerning the ruins of stately edifices yet remaining amongst them, the melancholy monuments of their former grandeur and long-lost science, they always answer that they were built by magicians."

I know it is hard to imagine a world in which we see responsibilities as opportunities, not obligations, and freedom as something you use, not as something you lose. But there are stately edifices for us to build, and mansions in the sky, and we can be magicians too.

A promissory note to love

I remember being involved with a man who always seemed to be saying nice things to me yet something didn't feel quite right. "You are wonderful," he'd say. "I can always count on you to understand." Or, "I want to thank you for being so patient." Or, "I love you for not getting angry. My ex-wife would have blown her stack." And I would puff up with pride and be patient or forgiving again for a day or two no matter how hard it was on me. And then one day I figured it out and I said to him, "I don't want to be patient any more. And I don't want to be impatient either. I want to be treated fairly. And I don't want any more points for denying my needs."

It takes a while to learn when you are being

bought off with ego balm, a while to learn that if both don't win everyone loses. And longer still how to protect both of you, not just yourself or them, so no one gets chipped or intruded upon and the bad habits of one don't dictate the terms for both.

There are people who make you crazy and then blame you for so being, and others who make you afraid to speak in case you precipitate a crisis far greater than the one you are trying to discuss, and still others whom you have to consider your zen project and declare yourself a saint, but it is really all the same—one person acting in reaction to another, two people whose behavior supports the wrong being done to both. A relationship that isn't being nourished so neither participant can thrive. Two people who are robbing the same bank and wondering where the money has gone.

And while one might be happier to think of oneself as a patient person than an impatient person or somebody who is calm rather than somebody who is hysterical, neither is much of an improvement over the other if both perpetuate the problem and neither turns it around.

And when you think of it, it is also true that none of us really wants to be forgiven. We all want to be thought well of, so forgiving might feel good to the forgiver but it doesn't feel good to the one who is forgiven, and in the end it is far kinder to help others understand what is needed so they can get to feel good too.

They've been making a pretty good case lately for sticking up for your rights but very little is said about the other part of the work, making sure the other person's rights are looked after too, and when you are talking about a relationship, their rights are as important to you as yours. So if you get stuck in a place where you are always defending yourself, or pacifying them or being manipulated, or doing a little manipulating yourself, you are on the enemy's side, helping to bring about your own doom. Because there can't be two sides in a relationship, only one, and everyone who is thinking them or me has to learn to give that up.

There is always duality in a relationship, always contradiction. The Greek myths try to teach us that, by exacting heavy penalties from those who try to simplify reality by denying contradictions. Even the fairy tales try to warn us that the bad and beautiful are always with us when they portray the prince as a frog and the princess as old crone, although they always hold out the promise that we can change that once and for all with the right combination of words and deeds, and I think that is where they go wrong.

Conflict is for me a sign of caring, as certain as if you are saying, you are worth it for me to be who I am, so I am not withholding myself. No one can be real if they keep themselves to themselves, so the greatest risk is not to risk. And the second greatest risk is not to let the person whose love you seek be themselves.

Real life is very different from a fairy tale that ends when the frog becomes the prince and never becomes a frog again, and the old crone is transformed into the beautiful princess before our astonished eyes. In real life they change back and forth from day to day. That is just the beginning of the story and what happens after is the tale. And the only thing that matters is if you can love them as they are, and they can love you back.

So you can pray to the giver of graces, and ask that he guide your path. But I wouldn't waste time praying for the perfect person to commit to, or help in making the decision as to where and when to commit. I'd pray for wisdom to help you learn how to give yourself, and lessons in how to enjoy another, and maybe a little help with finding a way to transform the contempt that comes with familiarity into an intimacy that breeds respect, because that's what you need to master the art of cherishing and hence get cherished yourself.

Monogamy is the art of making someone feel special so that they can make you feel special too. And so it involves the task of scaling the secret staircases till you reach the place where they've hidden their heart and you have hidden yours. And on the way slaying the dragons that guard the doors of both. The dragons of indecision and inadequacy, or expectation and misconception, the dragons of illusion and delusion, the dragons of blindness and boredom, of negligence and need.

And this getting to know another, and getting to know yourself, in ways too profound, too revealing ever to be plumbed outside of love, is the most daring work I know. And those who think of it as sheltered and lacking in imagination know not of what they speak. It takes far more emotional courage to lay open your heart to another, more fortitude to unmask another and find ways to enjoy the person who is there, than it ever does to dance away and cry defeat.

There are people who believe that everything is a slow wind down from the days of grand passion to the poor thin thing of everyday. And insist that if a fairy godmother offered them three wishes, they'd wish for the prince or princess of their dreams. But I know they'd be wasting their wish as those in fairy tales almost always do. The job is not to change the love object into another, but the eyes that do the seeing into the eyes of love. And to change the concept of commitment from something you make to the perfect object to something you make to perfecting yourself.

When people talk about commitment this is the work they mean, whether they know it or not. It's true it takes a certain intelligence and a generous spirit, and occasionally a bravado that you do not feel, but most of all it takes a willingness to take it on. To accept it as the work that must be done, interesting work when you think of it and no harder than most. And daily work, not seasonal or special occasion work. Work that must be done each and every day. But that's its special charm. If you do your work right, you should never be unemployed.

"It's not a having and a resting but a growing and a becoming," Matthew Arnold wrote in an essay called "Sweetness and Light," meaning that life is a process rather than a station you arrive at, and so, of course, is love. And so when you make a commitment, a declaration of loyalty, and a pledge of loving conduct, it is a promise to honor the other person so that they can honor you, and hence is a commitment to a way of proceeding, and a commitment to yourself as much as it is to them.

Commitment doesn't just mean to stay with someone through thick and thin. It means to make something work, and to help it keep on working, so each of you can trust yourself to the other in that private place, knowing that the other will do what has to be done, whatever that something is. And knowing that you always have the spiritual margin to get derailed again, and yet still grow old together with everything intact.

"I am," Thomas Wolfe wrote in *Look Homeward Angel*, "a part of all that I have touched and that has touched me, which having for me no existence save that which I gave to it, became other than itself by being mixed with what I then was, and is now still otherwise, having fused with what I now am, which is itself a cumulation of what I have been becoming. Why here? Why there? Why now? Why then?" Why not? one almost wants to add.

Whatever it is that asks you to believe in life comes from being needed, comes from feeling your value in another's eyes, and while a family fabric is a wanton weave of wants which often threaten to take you over, the pact you make with others to protect them protects you as much as it does them. And when you collude with someone to let them lay a claim on you, you cherish yourself as you cherish them.

I know some people talk about the first days of love as if they are the best, as if what follows later is just the time you must put in, the price that must be paid for the day that was seized way back when you were young, but there is something about the dailiness which to me is the most seductive of all—more addictive than languorous nights, more tempting than borrowed love. And almost anyone who has had it once will tell you its sights and sounds, its smells and its sensations resonate long after the stolen moments have faded, and that they pull at you like an undertow even when you wish they'd go away.

"I'm not ready to make a commitment," I hear people saying, meaning that they want to be able to leave if things get tough. Or that they don't think this relationship is perfect enough to warrant that kind of investment of themselves. I understand these feelings. I have had them myself. But making a commitment isn't giving something up. It is becoming something more. And as such it is its own reward. Not something contingent on someone else. I know that isn't ever really clear until you do it. And that it's hard to see how you can commit to another human being and get not them but you. I know it's hard to see how that could happen. But it is nevertheless still true.

There is a wonderful children's story called *The Little Prince* written by Antoine de Saint-Exupery about a little prince who lives by himself on a tiny planet which is quite barren except for two volcanoes and a rose. The little prince loves his rose and looks after it very carefully. He waters it daily and builds a fence around it to make sure that caterpillars won't eat it in the night. Then one day a space ship comes and takes him to earth and there he sees millions of roses just as beautiful as his, and for a moment he is very sad. "My rose is not unique. It is not the most beautiful rose in the universe," he thinks to himself. "I was a fool to love it." Then suddenly he realizes something. "Just a moment," he says to himself. "I don't love my rose because it is the only rose or because it is the most beautiful rose of all. I love it because I have looked after it. And nothing can change that." And with that the little prince flies back to his planet anxious to be with his rose once more.

An old gardener once said to me, standing over his sweetpea border, its various pinks and purples all rippling in the summer wind, "You plant and water and mulch and weed and water and mulch and weed again season after season, and what do you get? A froth!" And I laughed with him knowing what he said was true of love as well as flowers. It takes a lot of mulch, love does, to produce a froth.

12

To see the whole spread out against the sky

I have a little silver Georgian spoon in my sugar bowl and every time I pick it up and dip it into the sugar, I think of the woman who gave it to me and the fact that she isn't here any more. She died a couple of years ago by her own hand after growing depressed at the failure of her second marriage. Her first husband had gone out to get a newspaper one evening and never come back. His lawyers called the next morning to tell her that he wanted a divorce. Her second, an architect she met on a beach holiday, started seeing others shortly after their marriage. She barely survived the first but the second was too much for her, with his betrayal went everything she ever dreamed about, everything she ever wanted.

Every time I pick up the little silver spoon she gave me I get mad at her. Mad at her for letting them get to her, mad at her for not realizing her life was too precious to throw away because it didn't seem to be working at the moment. Mad at her for letting their judgment of her become her judgment of herself. And mostly mad at her for not remembering it's not over till the fat lady sings.

Most of us have thought from time to time when life conspired to let us down that this was surely the last quarter of the moon and all was lost or losing. And looked about us wondering why everyone seemed to have what we had not and why they did not seem to pay the price we did, and how they blundered into peace when we had lost the way.

I'll admit to thinking thoughts like those, to often being someone who concerned myself more with what I wanted than with what I had. Someone who spent a lifetime learning that perfume is what flowers throw away, and I had what to throw away too, and when the gods don't give you what you hoped for, they often give you something else instead.

Somerset Maugham wrote a story about an old man who was a verger in a church called St. Peter's, Neville Square, for many years and when the church got a new vicar the old man was called in and fired. "We can't have a verger who can neither read nor write," was all he was told. The old man was very distressed and went out into the street, dazed and confused, and walked and walked not knowing where he was going or what to do with himself. All he really knew was that he needed some pipe tobacco but there was no tobacconist to be found. Finally it came to him that he should open a tobacco store, which he did. And it prospered and after a while he opened another, and another. One day he was taking his earnings to the bank and the bank manager came over and asked him to sign his deposit slip. "I can't read or write," the old man explained. "You can't read or write!" the bank manager exclaimed, as if repeating the impossible. "Good God, man! What would you have been now if you had been able to read and write?" "I can tell you that," said the old man. "I would be the verger of St. Peter's, Neville Square."

It's hard to tell our bad luck from our good luck sometimes. Hard to tell sometimes for many years to come. And most of us have wept copious tears over someone or something when if we'd have understood the situation better we might have celebrated our good fortune instead.

"Our true honor is not to have a great part, but to act it well," Samuel Johnson said, adding, "That virtue only is our own—and that happiness always in our power." That is something to keep in mind these days when many of us won't get the life we expected, and the life that expected us will get somebody else. And sometimes nobody at all.

There is an Aesop fable about a cock who finds a pearl and tosses it aside as he is hoping for a barley corn instead. So many of us are like him, staying with our loneliest thoughts and our purest prayers as if they were the only game in town.

I knew a girl once who had been going with a fellow for a very long time who never popped the question, and she was getting very anxious. And finally she went to a fortune teller who told her she would get a diamond ring very soon, and to be patient as there wasn't long to wait. So she waited for another six months. Then one day her number was called at a raffle, and she won first prize—a diamond ring. And no one could fathom her behavior when she threw her prize on the ground and stomped on it, and ran screaming from the room.

I do not mean to make light of this, and neither did the girl when she told me about it several years later, with a candor that respected herself as much as the tale she was about to tell, only to say she understood one can never change the past, only the hold it has on you, and while nothing in your life is reversible, you can reverse it nevertheless.

Self-respect and expectations and love and commitment are all rolled up together in most of our minds. And the lives we get and the actions we take have a lot to do with how we view them. And so does how much of what we want we believe to be within our grasp, and how much of it we think must come from someone else.

But there are always two things we can give ourselves. Peace and joy. Peace in the knowledge that we have value, because we have things to give, and joy in our receptivity to the world, to everything it has to offer. Even that which we would have gladly skipped but from which we reached another place.

And it is our privilege to apply to our lives the attention we would apply to an unfinished work, not ritualizing the idea of an ultimate solution, or assuming anyone's attitude or allegiance, but working all the time at our capacity to endure, through the updrafts and the downdrafts, full of wonder at life's complexity, at its fierceness, and at its surprises.

"The things of life might be over prized and treated as final when they are not," wrote Epictetus. "They bear to life the relation which inns bear to home. As if a man journeying home, and finding a nice inn on the road and liking it, were to stay for ever at the inn. Man has forgotten thine object, thy journey was not to this, but through this."

One can look for happiness in sex, in others' approval, in appeals to magic, or one can find it in growing, understanding that you will take two steps sideways for every step forward that you make. And accept the fact that life is like fording a river, stepping from one slippery stone to another, and you must rejoice every time you don't lose your balance, and learn to laugh at all the times you do.

All of life is a learning experience. Learning how to see ourselves and others in a kinder, gentler light, learning how to see life not so much as a box but as a river, learning how to juggle your own frailties and those of others with equal care, learning that helping someone love themselves is a far better way to get love for yourself than demanding that they love you and skulking about when they don't.

There is a Hasidic story that I like about a rabbi who rejected a bribe offered to him by a prominent member of his congregation and, very pleased with himself, told this to the Zaddik, who was his teacher and his master, with a self-satisfied air. But the Zaddik, instead of congratulating him, blessed him and expressed the hope that he would become an honest and a God-fearing man.

The rabbi was disappointed and not wanting to offend the Zaddik said, "I am delighted with the blessings of my teacher and master and what more could I ask? But why did you wish me this just at this time?"

And the Zaddik replied, "God has mercy when he leads every man into temptation befitting his inner level. The common man into petty, the superior man into grave temptation. The fact that you were exposed to so slight a temptation is a sign that you have not yet reached the upper rungs to perfection. That is why I blessed you, asking God to let you ascend to them and be found worthy of a greater test."

I wish for all of us the same blessing, my reader. I wish that we might master the art of giving love both to ourselves and others, and that we might come to truly understand that you really own in this world only what you can give away, without having to ask for anything back, and so never feel tempted to beg for love again. And that we be soon worthy of a greater test. Another opportunity, if you will, to challenge ourselves.

"Two gates for ghostly dreams there are, one gateway of honest horn and one of ivory. Issuing by the ivory gate are dreams of glimmering illusion, fantasies, but those that come through solid, polished horn may be borne out, if mortals only know them," Homer wrote in *The Odyssey*.

And that is what I guess this life is all about. Getting to understand one's dreams and know them for what they are. The hopes of children wanting to be admitted to the company of adults, the fears of the vulnerable wanting to become strong.

"We shall not cease from explorations," T.S. Eliot wrote, "and the end of all our explorations will be to arrive where we started and know the place for the first time."